Judie has been many things in her time: heating engineer, telesales person, Tupperware agent/manager, hot lingerie demonstrator – that was fun! – choir mistress, probation worker, folk singer and for 20 years a sailing instructor (which included cooking romantic dinners on a luxury yacht). She now spends her time cruising the canals on a 60' narrowboat with husband John and ship's dog Calamity, but that's another story…

Nothing at boarding school prepared her for such a life, but her experiences there gave her a strong self of survival and the belief that anything was possible.

This, her first book, is a miscellany of memories of seven formative years at a traditional girls' boarding school and will surely strike a chord with those sent away to school 60 odd years ago! And maybe give an insight of what it was like growing up in the post-war years when so many subjects just weren't mentioned and 'female things' were learnt from ones' peers who were equally ignorant!

Jo-Anne is an illustrator, living and working in the Bordeaux region of France. Amid the local vines, she refined her skills as a watercolour painter, exhibiting regularly throughout the region and winning several prizes for her pen and ink sketches.

She has illustrated children's books, the most recent, *Moffy*, was published last year.

For John, who has put up with all my foibles for over sixty years. Thank you, darling.

To Joan

An lovely dog walking companion.

Best wishes

Judie.

Judie Surridge and
Jo-Anne Surridge

AND BRUINY CAME TOO

AUSTIN MACAULEY PUBLISHERS™

LONDON • CAMBRIDGE • NEW YORK • SHARJAH

A CIP catalogue record for this title is available from the British Library.

ISBN 9781528918022 (Paperback)
ISBN 9781528962131 (ePub e-book)

www.austinmacauley.com

First Published (2020)
Austin Macauley Publishers Ltd
25 Canada Square
Canary Wharf
London
E14 5LQ

Thank you, Austin Macauley, for believing in me and for your patience and guidance over the past year.
To the school which made me the person I am today, warts and all.

Preface to Bruiny (1)

"You'd better write a preface," said my daughter, Jo. "You know, something historical to set the scene. After all," she added, "you are very old…"

As she had taken the trouble to read all the drafts, I had sent her over the past few months, I felt beholden to respect her advice. But what to write? The 1940s are obviously ancient history to anyone born up to 60 years ago, though much of it is crystal clear in my memory.

Things were just getting back to some sort of normality after the Second World War. We still ate copious amounts of carrots, not to better our eyesight but because my mother, along with every other parent who had gone through shortages and scarcity, had stored bags of the stuff in the outhouse. They stood in sacks alongside potatoes, also sacked, and a huge Ali Baba jar of isinglass filled with eggs. We were all hoarders of everything from old Christmas cards, cut up to make the following year's gift tags, to any outworn kitchen appliance, which may just come in useful at a later date.

All the more surprising then was the likelihood of going away to school with all the attendant expense and three-month separation from the family. Hull had been severely bombed during the war, London even more so, and I had just spent two very happy years at the local high school, newly returned from evacuation in the Lake District, for the duration of the war.

But the die was cast. I was going 200 miles away for nine months of the year to heaven only knows where – I certainly didn't! In theory, it was wonderful but, in the event, it was no Malory Towers as you will find out…

Memo from Jo. That's fine but prefaces are normally written in the third person and give some indication of the contents of the book.

Here goes:

Preface (2)

At nine and a quarter year old, Judy was preparing to go to boarding school. An avid reader of Enid Blyton's St Clare's and Malory Towers books, she was only too eager to experience life. What could be better than friends 24/7, midnight feasts, school outings and all the other, hitherto unknown delights? She was to find that reality bore little resemblance to fiction and her sole confidante was Bruiny, a chocolate coloured bear, bought the day before she arrived and who was constantly with her for the 7 years she lasted at the boarding school. To say she was a square peg in a round hole was to put it mildly – a very round peg unable to fit in a very small square hole would be a more apt description. But here is her account, warts and all, of daily life during her formative years.

Chapter 1
And Bruiny Came Too

The year was 1947.

I was nine and a quarter year old.

Rationing was still with us, as was the need to carry an identity card at all times.

The brown wrapped parcel was sitting at my place on the table waiting to be unwrapped. It wasn't my birthday, I wasn't expecting a present, what was it and why was it there?

Not just any book

"Open it," invited Mum mysteriously. "You'll find out."

So, I did. Paper torn off in anticipation and strewn on the floor.

"Pick that up first," she ordered. I did. Always best to do what mothers say…

A book – not just any book but ' The First Term at Malory Towers' by Enid Blyton. I had eagerly devoured the whole of the St Clare's series about life at boarding school and was hoping for the Malory Towers books for the next few birthdays.

"Why?" Always best to find an answer if there is one. Also, I was of a curious nature and looked for any hidden agenda.

"You remember that little test you took last month at school, dear?"

It had been mentioned that there was some sort of paper with questions to answer, which I quite enjoyed doing, but my parents had mentioned it so casually I hadn't thought it was of any importance. It turned out that I had sat in the common entrance exam and done well enough to be accepted at any school, private or public, in the country.

The significance of the book became apparent when Daddy asked casually, "Would you like to go to boarding school?"

Well, who wouldn't? Stories of midnight feasts, eternal friendships, games of lacrosse – whatever that was – flashed through my subconscious. What a silly question! I couldn't wait to go away to school.

"Don't mention it to anyone yet, until we've got everything sorted out. It might not happen so keep it to yourself for the time being."

Naturally enough, the next morning at school assembly when the head mistress asked us if we had any news, I immediately waved my hand frantically in the air and announced to the entire school at the top of my voice. "I'm going to boarding school."

"Are you, dear?" asked Miss Jefferson puzzled. "Your parents haven't said anything about it."

Whoops, I had forgotten that she was a friend of my mother's and was coming to our house for morning coffee the next Saturday. Not a good start to a new venture. But as I found it really hard to contain my excitement, Miss J was telephoned that evening and all was in the open and I was forgiven.

Suddenly, all was rush and chaos to get ready to send me to heaven knew where to start a new life. The school my parents had chosen was a good public school near Watford. It was near enough to the capital for the brochure to assure parents that pupils would get a thorough knowledge of London, whilst we were there, and also Daddy really hoped that I would get rid of my Hull accent.

Large envelopes of information kept arriving through the post. Most of it didn't interest me, but then more packages were delivered from Peter Jones, a very upmarket clothes shop in London. They were the only stockists for the school uniform and as a result were VERY expensive. Parents' lips were pursed but the die was cast and clothes were duly ordered and delivered.

Then the booklet came. A very comprehensive catalogue of everything we would need to have with us. It started with the clothes list, which Mum perused very carefully. She tut-tutted quite a lot.

"Only two pairs of under-knickers? For three months it doesn't seem many." Then two bust bodices (bras to you and me!). As I was only nine years old, they seemed a little excessive but as they were itemised, she duly went out and bought the smallest she could. As I hadn't seen anything like them, I had a rapid lesson in trying them on and decided there and then that I was never going to grow bosoms or wear such odd garments.

The next item on the list was three packets of sanitary towels. What sort of towels were they? We didn't seem to have any in our laundry cupboard. Mum had thought and devoutly hoped that we would learn the facts of life from a biology teacher once we were at school. However, she was used to answering my questions and felt beholden to give me a lightning – and very basic – talk on the birds and bees. Soon afterwards, three odd shaped parcels containing looped padded sanitary towels were purchased, plus an elastic belt with hooks back and front to hold said towels. I then had an embarrassing lesson on how to wear these when necessary – UGH! I decided it was not for me and fervently wished I had been born a boy. They were duly packed. I made sure they were well hidden at the bottom of the trunk. No way was I going to do anything with them.

Great excitement when we had to go shopping for bits and bobs. Soap, toothpaste, flannel, brush, comb, hairgrips etc. were all available at the local Woolworths, spread out on counters before us in a bewildering display, and we returned home with a wash bag full of goodies. Mum had insisted on buying the largest bar of soap and tube of toothpaste, which she hoped would last me the whole 3 months.

Largest bar of soap and toothpaste

A week before term started, there was yet another delivery. This time it was a huge traditional school trunk – so exciting, just like Malory Towers. It had leather handles at each end and two lockable catches, plus attendant keys. Inside, there was a top tray, partitioned to take smaller items and shoes, and it looked enormous! It had to be, as we were expected to take four sheets and pillowcases, two handtowels and two bath towels with us. Luckily, when you are only nine and a quarter, clothes don't take up too much room and by dint of all the family standing on the lid, the trunk was eventually closed, labelled and ready to be picked up by carrier.

As it would not arrive at school until a few days after we did, we also had to have an overnight case with everything needed for up to a week. Even in those days, the arrival dates for luggage was a little vague! I acquired an expanding suitcase from an uncle, which held everything I could possibly need for a month's safari. I insisted on packing it myself and there were so many treasures I just had to take with me. When closed, it was far too heavy to carry so out came the dolls, jigsaws, books as yet unread, and in went a host of absolute necessities and it became manageable.

The last week of the holidays passed in a blur of frenzied activity. I visited the dentist, the hairdresser and finally all the relations living nearby to say my goodbyes. As I was the first in the family to go away to school, all uncles and aunts made a great fuss of me and I was overwhelmed with gifts of sweets (their rations) and extra pocket money. I accepted all gifts with an over exuberant hug and stowed everything into my newly acquired shoulder bag, also an item on the school list. Once we got home, Mum emptied the bag of all goodies, put the sweets into my sweet tin, item 34 on the list, and the money disappeared into Mum's purse.

My sister, Wendy, was five at the time. I'm not sure what she made of all the fuss, or was even aware of what was going on. She was also the recipient of relatives' largesse and was allowed to keep her sweets. Grossly unfair and I think I ate the majority of them for her, not the nicest memory of our last couple of days together.

Chapter 2

The big day finally dawned. For the first term, my mother was taking me to school rather than being put on a train in Hull and met in London by a member of staff. I don't think she trusted the arrangement, added to the fact that I had never been on a train before. We were to spend a night in London in a hotel then take a taxi ride to my new school. What an experience, I couldn't wait!

The train to London was at 9:15. This meant getting up at some ungodly hour. So much to do. Bath, hair wash, proper breakfast in case there was nothing to eat on the train, last minute packing and interminable snippets of advice which went right over my head but no doubt made my parents feel much better!

All the alarm clocks

As no one in the family was a morning person, we didn't come to till at least ten o'clock, Mum was worried that we would all oversleep and miss the train. Actually 'worried' was far too gentle a word for her anxiety, she became increasingly paranoid and duly prepared for every eventuality. All alarm clocks in the house were set for 6:30, neighbours were coerced into ringing up at ten-minute intervals till 7 o'clock and the telephone operator was briefed to ring at 7:15.

Arriving in London was a blur. We went straight to Hamleys toyshop as a treat and I was given the present money to spend. A whole pound! Riches indeed. We had nothing to compare with such a wondrous emporium in Hull and I spent ages wandering around such a magical store. It was huge and it is a testament to Mum's patience that she didn't hustle me round in 10 minutes. I finally spied a sad looking brown bear with one crooked eye just waiting to be loved, price £1 and that was it. Bruiny became mine. Naturally, he wouldn't fit into my new suitcase, we needed to get to know each other, and by the time we reached our hotel, I had told him my life history. He listened wisely and nestled in my arms.

A sad bear

The next day, we arrived at Happy Mount House, the most junior part of the school structure and we were welcomed by the senior mistress, Miss Minton, and shown around the house. Mum then left and I couldn't understand why she was sniffling. She said she was getting a cold but you don't have tears with a cold...

I was introduced to Mary; she had been at school for a year and was consigned to be my 'housemother'. That meant showing me the ropes and helping me for the first term to find my feet. A good system but unfortunately, Mary and I didn't see eye to eye on anything. She was from Potters Bar and derided my Hull accent. The more she scoffed the broader my vowels became – a vicious circle!

The first question I was asked was, "Where is your ration book and identity card?"

Where is your ration book?

Oh dear, they were in Mum's handbag as she didn't trust me to keep them safe. The staff had to ring her hotel for them and she duly brought them the next day, only stopping briefly to deliver them so she wouldn't miss the train home.

We were warned that the non-appearance of a ration book meant no meals till it materialised, but in spite of the lack of mine, I was allowed to have dinner. I had one slice of marmite on toast. The rest of the pupils were given sausages and beans. That was the first occasion I wished I was home again but it certainly wasn't the last.

Chapter 3

A word about Happy Mount House. Whoever named it must have had a wry sense of humour. There wasn't a hill in sight and as for merriment it was singularly lacking in all the time I was there.

It had been a large house of some quality, now adapted for two preparatory years before we advanced to junior and senior schools on a campus nearby. The two classrooms were ornate with high, fancy ceilings and huge fireplaces in which a fire never had occasion to be lit. There was central heating of a sort, a 4" diameter pipe ran around the rooms at floor level but gave out very little heat. No doubt it looked good on the prospectus though.

There were two staircases, one probably for the servants in times gone by. The front one led to three dormitories each housing six pupils and the servants' stairs took us up to the bathroom and toilets. Yes, bathroom in the singular. It held a monstrosity of a tub, large enough to bath an elephant and it transpired that we had baths in groups of four to conserve water. We had no proper curtains at the windows, they had not been replaced as the wartime blackouts still had a lot of life left in them. They completely shut out all lights, as indeed they were meant to, but it left the dormitory and landings in total blackness and rather frightening.

A monster of a tub

Mary took me in charge and showed me up to my dormitory, which I was to share with five other girls. As well as Mary, I met Julia, who I learnt later had an uncle who was married to a lady-in-waiting at the palace and as such she felt vastly superior to the rest of us. Sarah, Lisa and Helen made up the full complement, they seemed to hang onto every word that Julia uttered and were somewhat in awe of her. They had all been at the school for a year already and new girls were always fair game for ribbing. Julia sneered at my Yorkshire accent, pretending not to understand what I said, and the others laughed nervously at her snide remarks. I vowed to keep well clear of her.

As most of the pupils lived within driving distance, their trunks had been delivered and unpacked but my bedlinen was still in transit so the bed was made up with school sheets which had seen better days and were harsh and scratchy. Mary was in the bed next to me and asked if I would like to hear about the school in its former days. At bedtime, she regaled us with a lurid tale of a past murder in the servants' quarters with a subsequent ghost who walked the corridors after dark. She was a very good storyteller and I was terrified. I hid under the blankets, held Bruiny very firmly and tried to sleep.

I must have slept a few hours but woke whist it was still pitch black desperately needing a wee. There were no lights on anywhere and I was panic-stricken. All through the war, I had been comforted with a nightlight by the bed and was totally unused to being in the dark. Add to that was the dread of meeting the ghost on its nightly haunt. I lay as still as possible but the need didn't go away and in desperation, I gave way. A slow trickle escaped from between my legs then an uncontrollable gushing poured forth and the sheets and mattress were thoroughly soaked.

The next morning, I was petrified at what might happen. I lay very still when it was time to get up. Mary came to shake me and recoiled in disgust.

"She's wet the bed," she announced to everyone. "You are really disgusting."

I burst into tears, someone went to collect Matron and the others led by Julia, stood at the foot of the bed singing "Judy's wet the bed" to the tune of 'The farmer's in his den'. I can't remember being more ashamed and mortified – or less popular! It soon became the talk of the school and other girls avoided me pointedly holding their noses when they came near. It was unfortunate that my surname was Snelling. This was obviously shortened to Smelly, then Smellypoo and finally the nickname which stayed with me all my school life was simply Poo.

Matron took charge, changed the sheets and mattress and gave me a large red rubber cover to put under the bottom sheet in case of a recurrence. She also provided a china chamber pot, ornate with painted roses, which she put under my bed for future night-time emergencies. I was then taken to see Miss Minton and spent a most embarrassing ten minutes trying to explain that I didn't have a problem with my bladder, I hadn't wet the bed since I was two and it would NEVER happen again. I was too scared to tell her I was terrified of the dark and far too fearful to mention the wandering ghost. Miss Minton put the episode down to homesickness but said she had to write and tell my mother. My heart sank. What would Mum think? Would I ever live it down?

After breakfast, we all lined up outside the dispensary for inspection. Matron stood at the front of the queue and asked each one in turn, "Have you evacuated your bowels?"

What on earth did that mean? I turned to Mary who whispered, "She means 'have you done number twos', just say yes, you'll see why."

The girl in front obviously hadn't heard Mary's words of wisdom and answered, "No, Miss."

Wrong answer!

Out came a vile looking bottle of California syrup of figs and an equally disgusting phial of paraffin emulsion and she was given the dose of her choice to help future movements. Needless to say, after that nobody owned up to bowel non-function. There must have been a lot of constipated pupils that term.

Disgusting phial of paraffin emulsion

Chapter 4

So much to learn that first day. No formal lessons but a huge learning curve. Our pocket money was taken into safekeeping along with our sweet tins – mine almost empty already – and securely locked in the office. Mondays and Saturdays were sweet days, an allowance of t w o sweets per time. Queuing up after lunch for our ration on those days became a highlight of the week. Alas, it didn't last long. My tin seemed to empty very quickly, due no doubt to my sleight of hand secreting extra toffees up my sleeve and eating them guiltily in the toilet, in case anyone saw and reported me.

Our sweet ration

The following day, our trunks arrived and were placed at the foot of our beds. We were told to unpack everything and lay the contents on the bed for checking against the clothes list. My heart sank thinking of those three unmentionable packets at the bottom of the trunk, which I had to confront.

Matron was in charge of checking all items. She queried the bust bodices and looked at my completely flat body up and down in disbelief, but it all came apart when she saw the packets hidden under my sweaters. "Aah, that explains everything," she said.

What it explained I didn't know but I was then seen by the school doctor who asked the most embarrassing questions to which I didn't know the answers. I think Mum has a lot of explaining to do when I get home!

I was also totally embarrassed when my sheets were unpacked. All the other girls had pristine white cotton sheets while I was supplied with striped flannelette bedding. It was looked down on by them – after all, I was from the North with an accent to boot. But they never got lost in the laundry and nobody pinched them for their beds, when theirs had gone astray.

In my trunk were several items I did not recognise. One was a bag holding two brushes, a duster and tin of shoe polish. Saturday morning was shoe-cleaning time. We had four pairs of shoes to polish and I hadn't a clue how to start. I took advice from Mary – bad move! With a smirk, she told me confidently to put half the tin of polish on the duster and smear it onto the shoes. It was not a good introduction to keeping shoes clean and I acquired an order mark for messing up the bench with brown polish. Matron would not believe that I didn't do it on purpose. An order mark on the first week did not bode well for the future, especially as I felt very hard done by and it was totally unjust. At that time, I had no idea of the significance of an order mark, it was to loom large throughout my school life.

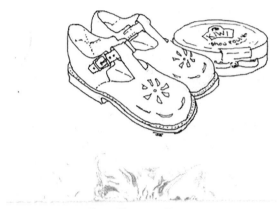

Shoe Cleaning Time

The matter of the gazunder just didn't go away. I refused point blank to admit it was there, but all the others in the dorm thought it was great fun to see if they could fill the blessed thing before morning. For two days, I didn't realise this and it wasn't until Matron smelled a nasty under the bed that I was told in no uncertain terms to get it emptied every night. I also got an order mark for slovenly behaviour and she would need notify to my parents.

I got my own back on the girls the following morning. They had excelled themselves and the pot was near to overflowing. All the slippers were in a rack by the door and as I went past I 'accidently' tripped. Oh dear! What a pity. I managed to soak all the slippers on the rack. I had taken the precaution of hiding mine under the bed. My popularity fell several notches and stayed well below zero for the rest of the term.

That day, we were assigned to one of four houses. It was under the umbrella of the three 'Cs'. Cohesion, Confidence and Competition. It was explained that our loyalties lay first to our classmates, then to our houses and lastly to ourselves. That way, we would become valued members of society and always think of others before ourselves. Any gold stars for exemplary behaviour would add to our house total and all order marks for bad behaviour would count against both class and house. There were cups awarded each term for nearly everything, house cups, form cups and best in year cup. To be given an order mark was a serious offence. All infringements were duly entered in THE BLACK BOOK and offenders listed prominently on a black rimmed board on the wall of the main hall for everyone to see and be shamed.

In itself, an order mark meant nothing, just a mark in THE BLACK BOOK, but it represented grave disapproval and threat of further punishment. What that further punishment was very few of us discovered. I was one of the elites, I was the first, and to my knowledge the only one, to have the slipper, the ultimate disgrace. I was made to lie on my bed on my front whilst Miss Minton gave me three whacks on my bum. I had taken the precaution of wearing all my pairs of knickers, two white underpants and two thick navy bloomers, so the pain was far less than my chagrin. My parents were also notified, which was a far worse punishment.

We were expected to have a 'hobby'. There was an hour set aside each evening for hobby time. This was yet another mystery which was solved when I found an embroidery kit in my trunk. My granny was an expert needlewoman and had provided a tray cloth and sewing equipment hoping I would get tuition at school. But we were largely left to our own devices and I never got the hang of fancy sewing. Mum didn't get her tray cloth for Christmas either!

Chapter 5

I adjusted to school life well enough on the whole. The food improved and I stayed clear of more order marks – and Julie and her coterie. Half term loomed and all was excitement as most of the pupils were going home for the long weekend. Only two of us were staying in school, Hull was too far to travel just for the weekend, but we were promised a good time with a member of staff who had stayed to look after us. I had received a ten-shilling note (50p) from my parents to treat myself over the weekend and life was looking good.

A ten-shilling note

It was even better when Miss Minton told me that Mum was coming to take me out the next day. She was in London with my father who was there on business and had the chance to come and see me. I actually only listened to

"…your mother is coming tomorrow…" and didn't take in "for a day out." I thought I was going home and flew upstairs to pack a case in readiness.

We had a great day together with lunch out and a visit to a local garden fête. When we returned back to Happy Mount, I went to collect my suitcase. Mum gently explained I was to stay at school but it would soon be Christmas and I would be home again. As we said a tearful goodbye, on my part this time, she whispered in my ear, "Promise me, darling that you won't wet the bed again."

I was totally mortified. I had forgotten that every untoward activity was reported back to parents and I ran inside the building, flung myself on the bed and wept inconsolably in Bruiny's arms.

The rest of the term went by in a blur. I achieved my one and only gold star, which raised my profile in class and house a little. We were asked to write something for the school magazine, due out the next term, and I remembered a poem I had written at my previous school. It was a prayer which actually scanned and rhymed, but Miss Minton didn't actually believe I had written it myself until confirmation came from my parents that yes, I could actually write poetry. It was duly printed in the 1948 issue and I was thrilled when it was adopted as the class prayer for the year. I can still remember it 71 years later and it went something like this

'May I, God, a little child says my prayer to you.
I know you listen to me, Lord, and other children too.
Thank you, God, for the sunshine. Thank you, God, for the rain.
Thank you, God, for all that lives, please keep them all from pain.
I shall always remember how Jesus died for me.
Your life was always perfect, please let me grow like Thee.'

Chapter 6

Homecoming loomed.

Excitement increased all around.

Preparations had been made. Packing in reverse, clothes on bed, checked by Matron, "How on earth can you lose all 24 handkerchiefs in one term?"

Actually, it was very easy. With no pockets in our uniform but a large one in our top navy knickers, it was the receptacle for everything we carried with us. No doubt in visits to the toilet many articles fell out of pockets and were flushed away. Also, a lot of my things mysteriously 'disappeared'. Not only hankies but pencils, rubbers, odd socks all seemed to vanish into the ether. Of course, nobody claimed to have found anything, it was obviously my carelessness and it was duly noted in THE BLACK BOOK. Packing completed, trunks were dispatched to home addresses and we waited agog for the end of term. I couldn't wait to leave. Malory Towers had a lot to answer for. I had tried boarding school. Not liked it and looked forward to returning to my old school where I had friends who actually liked me.

The journey home was a new experience. First of all, we took a taxi to the station and then the tube to Euston. We were then marched in a crocodile through the streets of London to King's Cross to catch the LNER train to Hull. Bruiny, as always, was cradled in my arm, the other hand clutching not only a very heavy suitcase but a paper bag with sandwiches for lunch and a book to read on the journey. We were entrusted with our own train tickets, which on reflection seemed a little risky, given my propensity for getting things wrong, but on that occasion, all went well and six hours later, I was in my parents' arms and home again.

On Christmas Eve, a brown envelope arrived through the letterbox. I recognised my own handwriting and blanched inwardly. The week before term ended, we were instructed to address the envelope to our parents, which would contain my school report and I dreaded what the contents might say.

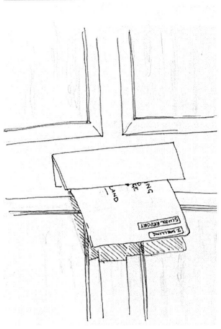

My school report

In the event, it wasn't too bad. I had actually managed to come top of the class by the end of term without exerting myself unduly. It seemed that I had covered most of the work at my previous school so it wasn't too hard a task. There was a cryptic note from Miss Minton about my inability to be a team player, a sentiment which was echoed each term throughout my school life. As we hadn't played any games in any teams, I was unsure what she meant but my parents took it very seriously. It didn't spoil the holidays however and I looked forward to resuming my education back in Yorkshire in the New Year. I had also lost any trace of a Hull accent much to my father's delight.

Chapter 7

New Year came and went. In early January, Mum brought my trunk in from the garage. I looked on in horror, I had never wanted to see it again. Maybe she was cleaning it to sell. I had no further need of it as I was sure I was returning home for good.

Realisation dawned when the dreaded clothes list appeared. I stopped Mum in her tracks as she began to sort out socks, vests and stuff. "I'm not going back you know," I stated, trying to keep my voice steady. "I've tried it and I prefer my old school."

Mum stopped in her tracks. "Don't be silly, of course you are going, darling, it's a lovely school and you did so well last term."

"How long must I go for?" I asked tearfully.

"Well, until you're 16, I suppose," she replied. "Till you've taken all your exams."

I recoiled in horror. That was a lifetime away but Mum was adamant and packing went ahead. This time the bras and sanitary towels were left at home.

The letter from Matron must have had some effect.

A week later, on time thanks to friends, alarm clocks and the operator, we were at Hull station to catch the 9:15 to King's Cross. I was delighted to see friends who were also dispatched to various schools in and around London. They all seemed very cheerful and had obviously settled into boarding school life quicker than I had.

****

A week later, we all went down with heavy colds. We must have been a disgusting lot as hankies were soon in short supply and noses were wiped on our sleeves, which became stiff and snotty hard over the week. Matron dosed us all with cod liver oil tablets, which we pretended to swallow then hid them in our knicker pockets.

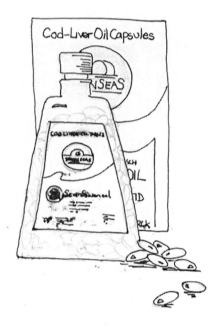

Cod liver oil

I was no more popular this term and came in for a lot of teasing. One morning, I found a row of the dreaded cod liver oil tablets taped under my desk lid just before a lesson. No time to extricate them and as the English mistress entered, we all stood up and the girl behind me slammed my desk lid down. The smell was vile. I felt really sick, but far worse was the mess made of my textbooks from the escaped oil. Miss Jones became aware of the aroma wafting from my direction and came to investigate. I then got one order mark for messing up my desk, another for ruining a textbook and a third for not swallowing the wretched pills. I was really incensed at the unfairness of it all, but the cardinal rule was that you never ever sneaked – if you did, you were the lowest of the low, so I said nothing and spent the next playtime cleaning my desk. It did mean that my house came bottom that week. I was definitely NOT a team player…

Teasing took many forms and, at nine years old, was not at all subtle. Crayons were broken before art class, textbooks went missing unaccountably and when they were found in my locker, there were ink stains on the pages. I was really taken to task on this last misdemeanour and my parents were billed for the replacement books. But I was too scared to sneak, Julie was well aware of that and her group tried to see how far they could go to make my life a misery.

There was a new girl in the bed next to mine, now minus red sheet and rosebud potty, thank goodness. Her name was Cynthia and it was her first time away. She was very homesick and cried into her pillow most nights. I would have lent her Bruiny for comfort but mine were the only tears he could share. She talked about running away and had even stashed the last few days' sandwiches in her drawer to eat on the way home. They looked most unappetising but better than starvation! She wasn't sure how long it would take her to get to Barnett.

"Will you come with me?" she pleaded one evening. "I can't go alone and you will look after me so well."

Flattery and friendship were scarce at that time and it seemed a great idea. I was as homesick as she was and the thought of returning home was irresistible, so I said yes and we made plans to escape. Down the fire escape, along the drive, wait at the bus stop and travel straight to her house. There were more than a few flaws in our arrangement. The fire escape was kept securely locked.

Heaven knows how we would have fared in the event of a fire – the drive was dark and forbidding, maybe the ghost haunted there as well, and we had no money for the bus fare. We did have a week's supply of spam sandwiches, rather stale and curled at the edges. What I was expected to do when we arrived at her home, I had no idea. I hoped my parents would come to my rescue and take me home for good.

In the event, it was a non-starter. The night we had planned our flight there was a terrific thunderstorm. There was no moon, no way to get out of the building and on my part, a great reluctance to go ahead with such a scatter-brained scheme. One of the few sensible decisions I made that term. Thank goodness she dropped the idea and the sandwiches were flushed down the toilet.

By the end of the school year, I was resigned to staying put. I did very little work and scraped through all tests with the minimum of effort. My reports did not make good reading and I grew to dread the familiar envelope dropping through the letterbox. I tried all ways to avoid that. I put the wrong address on the envelope, forgot the stamp, and spilt black ink over the address on various occasions. To no avail, a different envelope arrived spot on time and Bruiny and I hid in my bedroom until the report was read.

You ask why I never said anything to Mum and Dad about the teasing I endured. The simple truth was that it was so good to be home, I was able to put it behind me and returning to school, I was the eternal optimist and thought that this term it will be OK.

Chapter 8

Our class moved up to junior school, a vastly different ballgame. We were no longer the babes of the school and were expected to behave accordingly. At the first assembly, Miss Gillet, the senior mistress, told us of new beginnings. The past should stay in the past and we would start the New Year with a clean slate. I am sure she looked me straight in the eye as she said those words and I vowed to live up to her high standards.

What became of that solemn vow I am not quite sure but it wasn't long before I was in trouble again. It started innocuously enough in the bathroom the first evening. As usual, I had the largest bar of soap available from Woolworths and the biggest bottle of shampoo. Somehow between bathroom and dormitory both disappeared and I never saw them again. Julia perhaps? So, for the next few weeks, I washed without soap and shampoo. There must have been quite a pong following me around and it came to Matron's notice. The result was that each morning I had to go and collect a bar of strong- s m e l l i n g carbolic soap from the dispensary, wash myself thoroughly and return it after use. This arrangement palled after a very short while and I reverted to water and pong. I actually preferred that to the whiff of carbolic soap but classmates didn't and I was again ostracised.

Talking of washing and baths, there was a bath rota which was strictly adhered to. There were three bath times allocated per day, one bath per week per pupil. No wonder we all smelled a little – or a lot... My bath was first thing in the morning for the first term, on Tuesdays. The only good thing about that was that the water was still hot. Those who had afternoon or evening baths were lucky if the water was lukewarm.

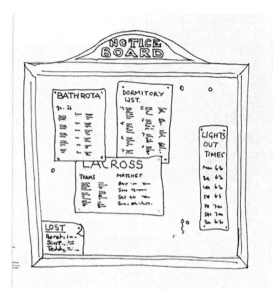

One bath per pupil per week

****

We were allowed to receive parcels from home and recipients were read out at lunchtimes, to collect from the staffroom after break. My grandpa once sent me a cardboard box full of crab apples from his garden. I adored crab apples and we picked them together each year for Granny to make jelly. What he thought I'd do with about 200 of them I'm not quite sure, most of them were rotten when they arrived, and the juice and pulp were escaping onto all the other parcels. I was asked in no uncertain terms to make sure Grandpa kept his crab apples to himself in future.

Box full of crab apples

My grandparents were Danish, a fact of which I was very proud. No one else had Danish blood in their veins and no one else had a grandfather who was an inventor. A downside of their nationality was that even though their English was fluent, they felt that their written letters weren't good enough to send and I never received one from them.

Later that term, I had a letter from Mum to say that Grandpa had died peacefully in his sleep and I shouldn't be too sad. It must have been a very difficult letter for her to write. I had no idea how to react, no one I knew had died before, but I felt sure that some show of sorrow should be the order of the day. So, I sat on my bed clutching Bruiny and cried very loudly until a member of staff noticed and came to see what was wrong. Mum then got a letter to say how badly I had taken my grandfather's death and would she please not send such news in a letter in the future. That upset her far more than me.

Miss Amos was the junior games mistress, a large lady with a throaty laugh, which she used often. I liked her very much; I also liked games very much, which helped, and one day to pay her a compliment, I said she had a laugh

39

just like my granddad – the other one. Unfortunately, she thought I was insulting her and another order mark was added to my total.

I also got an order mark for cheek. I had done some minor demeanour and Miss Gillet said severely, "Judy, that is just not done."

I replied in all innocence, "But it must be, I've just done it."

Best not to take what teachers say too literally, it can lead to all sorts of misunderstandings.

Chapter 9

That summer term, almost all the girls were infested with the dreaded nits! Oh, the shame of it. Drastic action was taken whether you were nit free or infected. I had no idea what a nit was and spent some time in the school library's biology section looking them up. Nasty little things which crawled around our heads, laid eggs and caused endless scratching.

Infected with the dreaded nits

I was justly proud of my research and lost no time informing everyone who would listen about the life cycle of a nit. This had an unfortunate effect which rebounded on me.

"How come you know all about nits?" Julia sneered and her throng joined in obediently. "Of course, you've had them before, you must have brought them with you. That's what happens when you live in the north."

Cue sniggers from her clique. Julia continued, "You do know we wash our hair regularly here, don't you? Is every one dirty up there?"

More snorts of laughter. It was soon relayed to everyone in our class that I was totally responsible for the infestation and I was yet again ostracised. Nobody listened to my explanation, the story was far more entertaining and I kept quiet and seethed inside at the unfairness of it all.

All access and egress to and from the school was banned, parents were not allowed to visit, but if they had they would have seen a weird sight. Our hair had been smeared with some special gunge and heads swathed in turbans. This gave the effect of a clutch of charladies without aprons but it did have the desired effect and we were rid of nits by the end of term.

Before the end of term, we were given 'the talk'. Our embarrassed form teacher was given the task of explaining all necessary facts of life to a giggly lot of 10-year-olds, a task which she whisked through at the speed of light. Suffice to say we were not much wiser by the end of it, but some things remain etched in my memory forever.

She produced a sanitary towel from a bag and an elastic belt and proceeded to show us how to use it – not literally, I hasten to add, that would have been a move too far. I knew that bit anyway. She then told us why we had periods but not that they were messy, inconvenient and the towels would leak at inappropriate moments. We had never heard the word 'menstruation' before. It sounded dire and we thought it must be an illness. It was always referred to as 'the curse' once we realised, we would all have to endure it. It was one of those unmentionable subjects only spoken about in undertones and then only when absolutely necessary.

Her other mantras included the following:

"Do not sit on the seat of public toilets, you might catch something." No explanation what that might be, but we all practised standing up to wee. There were a lot of wet toilet seats, boys were obviously better designed for that job!

"Never speak to a stranger." In Yorkshire, we talked to everybody, but apparently down south anything could happen. Again, we were not told what it might be and imagination ran riot.

Occasionally, she was taken off guard from her practised spiel.

"Why can't you say 'fuck'?" innocently asked one girl. "My uncle says it all the time, but Daddy says it's a bad word. What does it mean?"

Another word we hadn't heard before, must look it up in the dictionary.

Luckily, that question remained unanswered; the bell mercifully rang before our teacher had to elaborate. Periods: we had learnt about and what parents hadn't told us, we gleaned from lurid discussions after lights out. But as to how babies were conceived, we were still in the dark. The description of the sexual act had been glossed over in one sentence. All we knew was that somewhere in a bag were the wherewithal to make babies and a man kept it behind his private parts.

As no one in our dormitory had a brother, we were unaware what those private parts consisted of. I had a year-old boy cousin who I had bathed once or twice, but for the life of me, I couldn't see how his little button of a willy could do anything unmentionable. Boys to us were a foreign country and remained so all our school life. We had no contact with the opposite sex; all our teachers were ladies, unmarried for the most part, as they were the pre-war generation and only the head gardener was a man. As he was nearing retirement age, he didn't count and our knowledge of the male sex was mainly gleaned from romantic novels. We had long discussions after lights out as to whether boys had periods too and if not, why not.

Chapter 10

Illness of any sort was looked upon as a weakness, so most things went unreported until grazed knees became infected, colds became flu and a stay in the school sanatorium ensued. There was a very good reason for this in our eyes. The surgery was an open room with a screen available if you needed to be privately examined. Otherwise, everyone waiting knew exactly what ailments you were suffering from. Also, the normal practice of treating cuts, boils and the like was a boiling hot kaolin poultice slapped on the affected area and bandaged securely, so the badness could be extracted. An extreme form of torture to be avoided at all costs.

I developed what I thought was a boil on my bottom in rather an embarrassing place and after enduring great discomfort for a week, I really needed to see Matron to get it seen to. It must have been really painful as the idea of hot clay slapped up my behind offered relief in spite of the scalding.

"What's the matter with you, Judy?" she asked offhandedly, obviously thinking I'd cut my finger or something innocuous.

"I think I've got a boil, Matron," I muttered very quietly, hoping the full waiting room would ignore me. Not a chance! Ears pricked up, visions of squirting puss and screams of pain were too good to miss and the full complement in the dispensary listened with bated breath. They were not disappointed.

Listened with bated breath

"Well, where is it then?" asked Matron impatiently. "I haven't got all day, you know."

I didn't dare say where in earshot of everyone but silently pointed to my rear. She was good enough to bring out the screen, at which point ears pricked up even more expectantly from those in the queue and I duly bent over so she could examine my backside.

"You dirty, little girl, you've got piles." she exclaimed at top volume. Cue sniggers from audience. "You were told never to sit down on public toilet seats. Now see what you've got."

My shame was immeasurable. I was sent for a bath, given some obnoxious ointment to rub on the affected part and told to keep myself clean! I suffered from piles from then on, too embarrassed to mention it to anyone. It didn't do much for my popularity either.

Chapter 11

As in all well-run institutions, our school was governed by rules. They covered everything from a 24-hour timetable to the hour at which we went to bed and lights were out. We were in bed by 7:30 p.m. – unbelievable now but it was the norm then and we were used to going to bed whilst it was still light.

Stopping us talking after lights out was almost an impossibility for the staff member on evening patrol. She would enter the dormitory unannounced and ask, "Who is talking?"

I had been brought up to tell the truth so answered, "I was."

Nobody else opened their mouths, so I was the one collecting the order mark. This became a frequent occurrence with the teacher coming in and eventually asking, "Judy were you talking?"

I couldn't deny it, my voice was loud and easily recognised. How she thought I had carried on a conversation with myself in six different voices, I never asked, but it just added more order marks to my total.

Eventually, order marks became meaningless. I had accrued a good tally and they had little or no effect. Two things happened to change the teacher's approach. The next time we were whispering, oh so quietly, she asked the usual question getting the usual response.

"Right," she said in stentorian tones. "Judy Snelling, get dressed and come with me, we'll see about you."

Was I scared? My heart beat wildly as I had no idea what was in store. I was taken to the staffroom, sat at a desk with pen and paper in front of me and told to write down all the school rules before I could return to bed.

What a let out! I had never actually read the school rules and consequently had no idea what they were.

Write down all the school rules

I thought of everything I had been in trouble for and wrote them down, followed by things I would have liked to do which I was sure would not be allowed. The list included:

I must not climb the apple tree and pinch the ripe apples. (They were sour.)

No reading in the dormitory. (Why ever not?)

I must not climb out of the dormitory window onto the flat roof after lights out. (I could read out there, it was still daylight.)

I must not leave the hot bath tap running (that had cost me an order mark when it overflowed and the water was stone cold for the next bathers. They thought I had done it on purpose, maybe I had…).

There were several more and the teacher looked over my shoulder as I wrote. Her only words were, "Aah, that's a new one." She was obviously a lot wiser by the time I got to bed and I couldn't break those rules anymore!

The next time we had a nocturnal visit, I owned up as usual, but instead of being punished I was held up as an example of honesty. She then gave all the others an order mark for silent deceit, smiled at me and closed the door. I was vindicated! It was a good feeling that lasted till the following day, when I found a saturated sponge mysteriously hidden between the sheets.

Chapter 12

I would do anything for a dare. I thought it would make me popular with the other girls and did not realise they laughed at me and not with me.

One evening after a dare including a five-barred gate and some barbed wire, I found blood running down my blouse. I had inadvertently knocked a large mole off its base on my shoulder and it wouldn't stop bleeding. Sensing a drama, I was surrounded and gawped at.

"My granny says you die if your mole bleeds," offered Julia in tones of great gloom. Others nodded sagely and I suddenly felt rather faint.

"How long will that take?" I asked fearfully.

"It's very sudden." All nodded in agreement and I felt increasingly unwell. "Perhaps you'll die tonight."

Full-blown panic set in. What was I to do? This was far too serious for Matron to deal with.

Julia took charge. "First of all, you'll have to make a will," she announced sombrely. "Then write a goodbye note to your parents telling them you love them." All nodded in agreement and Sarah went for pen and paper to make it official. They were so kind and attentive, I felt almost happy. I left my new fountain pen to Julia, my letter writing case to Sarah and all other worldly good to be shared amongst the other three. I held onto Bruiny; he was coming in the coffin with me. Then I wrote to Mum and Dad, a very short note stained with the tears I was shedding at the thought of never seeing them again.

"What do I do now?" I asked Julia, the self-appointed expert in all things fatal.

"We lay you out."

What on earth was that? Julia had just finished reading a murder mystery and knew all the correct procedure.

"Then we pray for you."

Perhaps you'll die tonight

It was a Church of England school and we had learnt to pray at the slightest provocation – and boy, did that fall into that category.

I duly lay on my bed, they covered me with a sheet and knelt around, hands together and head bowed and we intoned the Lord's prayer with great solemnity and sang the first verse of 'Abide with me'. After all, I was at death's door and deserving of such attention.

"Now you go to sleep and with any luck, you won't die in agony."

The last words I was destined to hear on this earth! How could I sleep knowing I would never wake up? But eventually, I did fall asleep and actually awoke the next morning much to my surprise. The mole was still bleeding through the mole hole. I decided I didn't want to die so went straight to see Matron to see if she could save me.

I poured out my tale of woe and she was surprisingly sympathetic. She actually put her arm around me and taken aback by this show of affection, I burst into tears and sobbed onto her ample bosom. She also promised to regain my treasures, which had already found their way into the other girls' lockers. They were taken to task for putting me through such an ordeal, my mole stopped bleeding and life resumed its normal course.

Chapter 13

The second year in junior school brought a few changes. We were put into long dormitories instead of sharing a room with five others. They held 10 beds along each side, each one with a private cubicle behind the bed. This consisted of a curtained off wooden partition just taller than head height, containing a chest of drawers and shelf to house our tin jug and basin. At last, we had a little privacy. After all, we were reaching puberty although, we were on the whole blissfully unaware of the fact. Water for washing had to be collected in the jug from the sluice and the basin emptied after use. The easiest way was to pour the water back into the jug and leave the contents until the next wash time. If found, this invariably led to an order mark but it was worth it to save the extra trek down the passage.

The top of the partition walls made a fine springboard for jumping onto our beds. A favourite game was 'shipwrecked', where we had to traverse the length of the room and back again without touching the floor, using all parts of the furniture. The winner was one who jumped onto the last bed from cubicle top, doing a somersault in the shortest time. As I was the one sleeping in that bed, the springs invariably weakened and in due course gave way completely.

Naturally, this came to Matron's attention very soon and I was taken to task yet again. My punishment for the rest of the term was to sleep on a mattress on the floor while the bed was being repaired. Actually, there was not a lot of difference in the comfort and my bed wasn't bounced upon again.

****

Another difference was that we were encouraged to have pets at school. Quite an innovation and one of the few similarities to Malory Towers. The choice of pet one could have was rather limited, rabbits were the favourite, followed by white mice. One girl had a pet snake but they were banned after it escaped and caused chaos in the staffroom.

I desperately wanted a mouse to care for.

"Absolutely not," said Mum, who had a morbid fear of mice.

But I was determined and set about acquiring one. In the spring holiday I found an old orange box, a huge thing which would house a whole family of rabbits. I covered it with chicken wire and it made a perfect cage for my future companion. I labelled it with my name and school address and took it to the local post office to send off. All due credit to the postmistress, who didn't turn a hair when I told her proudly it was a mouse cage.

A perfect cage

I then sent a postal order for five shillings to the pet department at Harrods and asked them to send me two white mice, to arrive at school the day after the start of the summer term. Needless to say, neither cage nor mice made an appearance which was probably just as well!

Just before the end of term, six of us were summoned into Miss Gillet's office. What had I done now? I always seemed to be in some sort of trouble, if she wanted to see me. But this time was different.

"You six have the potential to be A star pupils, if you put your minds to it," she began. "Although you haven't shown much aptitude for work – yet. We are going to remedy that."

Groans from us thinking, *extra work? Ugh.*

"You are being transferred to a special class next term in the senior school where you will have individual tuition and hopefully exceed all our expectations."

WOW! How could I have managed that? My marks were less than mediocre most of the time, but as I didn't put in much effort that was hardly surprising. I determined to work harder the next term. Actually, that was my mantra every time my report came through the door each holiday, but I did mean it that time – really.

Chapter 14

Heavy grey serge skirt and jacket

All was changed that autumn. It started with the clothes list. Added to the normal items were thick black lisle stockings with attendant suspender belt, heavy grey serge skirts and jackets and lacrosse boots and stick. Due no doubt to the mass of carbohydrates provided for school meals and greed on my part, I had developed quite a rotund tummy. Mum was a little concerned and instead of a thin belt with delicate suspenders she swathed me in a ghastly roll-on, which covered me from waist to thigh. I looked better but prayed that no one would ever see it.

The boots and sticks were an unknown quantity, hockey was the game played in the north and we had no idea what to buy or where to purchase such items. Finally, Mum rang the school and I was able to collect them once term started. That was just as well as to carry a lacrosse stick across London, together with suitcase and Bruiny, was just asking for trouble.

Lacrosse, an unknown quantity

During the first week, we were introduced to 'accounts'. The first Thursday evening after supper, we gathered in the common room and were issued with an accounts book. Debits to be put on the left-hand side, incomings from the right. That first evening was a wakeup call. The left-hand side read:

School fund 6d (2 and a half p)

Library fund 6d

Breakage fund 6d

House fund 6d

Class fund 6d.

The right income column simply read £1.

That meant that after deductions we had 17s and 6d left to last us for 3 months. Add to that, 6d a week to put in the chapel collection and an obligatory 3d per week for the class newspaper and there wasn't a lot left for personal spending. But as we never left the school premises until we were seniors, it made little difference and gave us absolutely no conception of the value of money.

There were other changes too. A lot of activities and groupings were in our 'houses' and they became the focus of achievement in most areas of our school life. We had a housemistress in charge of each house, who oversaw all our activities. Miss Barmite was my housemistress and unfortunately, she and I seldom saw eye to eye over anything. She was a disagreeable lady of indeterminate age and uncertain temper. She had her favourites and I definitely did not come into that category.

I was in Nelson house, colour green, and we wore green ties to distinguish us from Darwin, blue, Raleigh red, and Drake, yellow. We also had grey berets with long tassels sewn on the top in our house colours. We had to sew our own tassels on and the proof of the quality of our sewing was how long they lasted when snatched off our heads and twirled round. Needless to say, mine came in for a lot of twirling and much resewing.

Order marks became much more of a serious offence. We were expected to have learnt from our junior days how to behave and they were only given out for serious breaches of discipline. Three in one week meant that you were expelled from your house and barred from all house activities. I managed to acquire nine one week and was consequently banned for a whole year. Oh, the shame of it! No taking part in extracurricular house activities, no selection for teams, and worst of all, I was not allowed to wear my tie so all could see my ignominy! I never meant to be disruptive or cheeky, I was a very square peg in a round hole and just didn't fit in to the system. It's no wonder Miss Barmite kept a very close eye on me.

Chapter 15

It took a while to find our way around the various classrooms and outbuildings around the school. The science lab was outside the main building, approached through the school laundry and across a corridor and I was late for the first chemistry lesson. Miss Howgood asked my name. I told her and she said grimly, "Yes, I've heard about you." Slight pause – "Where is your apron?" Naturally I had forgotten it, left it in my locker and spent the best part of the first science lesson getting lost going back to the main building. Not a good start…

The gym was also in the grounds and we kept our shorts, games blouse and gym shoes in a cotton bag, which we took there each period. Then came the crunch.

"All stockings off and shorts and shirts on please." From Miss Peebles. There were no changing rooms, we all stripped together, and long after everyone else had changed I was still wrestling with the wretched chastity belt! I wore it under my navy knickers for obvious reasons, so it was doubly awkward to remove it. There was great hilarity from the class, all were only too pleased to wrench it down my legs and only Cynthia thought to hold a towel around me to save complete embarrassment.

Once changed into proper gear, we then had to kneel down to check that our shorts were decorous enough. The hem had to touch the ground and woe betide any girl who fancied showing a bit of thigh!

In spite of a dubious beginning, I loved gym and became quite good at it. I had ditched the corset on gym days and held my lisle stockings up with elastic bands, which cut into the top of my legs. The stockings invariably ended up around my ankles but it was worth the inconvenience.

We were all checked at the start of each year to see if we needed 'remedial'. If you had flat feet, knock knees, round shoulders or a sticking out tum you had to attend the great hall on Monday evenings. You name it, they tried to remedy it! Yes, I joined the throng with my poor posture and was given various exercises to do each week to pull in my midriff. It would have been more effective to put me on a diet – or perhaps not...

We were marked each week on our deportment, A to E, and if you were an A for a whole term, you were awarded with a belt which was worn with pride. There wasn't anything for us E's to distinguish us, thank goodness.

With only six in our class, I fared much better that first term in upper school. I had friends at last and life was much happier. For the first time in three years, I had a best friend. Pam was my exact opposite. She worked hard, always handed work in on time, was excessively tidy and we complimented each other well. I would like to say she had a good effect on me but I'm not sure that was the case. But the six of us rubbed along well together in class and my marks improved – slightly.

Chapter 16

Food became a very important part of school life. As far as I was concerned, the whole day revolved around mealtimes. We were actually fed very well as long as you enjoyed stodge and copious slices of bread and marg!

We started the day at 7:45 with a hearty breakfast of cereals, something cooked and copious quantities of bread and jam. Then at 11 o'clock came morning break with hot cocoa and sticky buns – more of them later.

Lunch was the next highlight, where we filled up on a plentiful helping of meat of some sort with mounds of potatoes. We sat at long tables with a senior prefect at the head to dish out helpings. I tried to make myself indispensable to her by handing out plates and clearing the table in the vain hope of a larger helping of whatever was on the menu. Sometimes it worked and I steadily got fatter! There was a pudding of some sort every Sunday. The most frequent was bread and candied peel pudding with custard, naturally using up all the uneaten crusts from the previous day. We were not sure of the ingredients of the custard but it was hot and sweet and there was never any left in the jug.

We had afternoon tea at 4 o'clock, more thick slices of bread and marg washed down with mugs of tea and supper at 6:45, which was another cooked meal followed by yet more bread and marg. The bread came in long loaves, uncut and placed on the table ready for slicing by anyone who could cut straight. Wednesdays and Saturdays were red letter cake days, which were eagerly awaited. The cakes arrived in rectangular tins and were cut into the required number of slices by whoever was nearest the knife. Each piece was scrutinised to ensure that they were all a uniform size and we all had equal shares. It was a real bonus if someone was ill or away from our table and we got a larger portion. No wonder I put on weight during term time much to my mother's dismay. Thank goodness for games periods!

Chapter 17

Afternoons were given over to games lessons, which I really enjoyed. We were taught the rudiments of lacrosse and we learnt how to throw and catch a lacrosse ball in its odd shaped net, managing not to knock anyone's teeth out. I played in goal, much more fun than running up and down a muddy pitch. I think I was picked for that position because I filled the goalmouth better than the others! I was also a sitting target for the hurled ball. But I did get into the house team although we never won the lacrosse cup.

I did have my moment of glory however, when I was on the list for the school team and turned out for what was to be my debut and swansong in one. The reason I was chosen was not because of my brilliance as goalie but because the regular player had flu and I was the only one left who was available. Our opponents were from the local co-ed boarding school and were much rougher than we were.

After a terrifying first half in which they scored 12 goals to our measly one, I was confronted by their chief striker, evil grin on her face, galloping towards me with stick and ball waving menacingly above her head. She even had time to shout, "I'll get you," before delivering the ball directly at my face. As there were no face guards to protect the goalkeepers at that time, I fled the goalmouth, the ball went in for goal number 13 and I refused to return to the match.

We finally lost by 23 goals to one and I was never asked to play for the school again. This was a pity as when we had home matches against other schools, there was always a team tea afterwards with cakes and sometimes biscuits as well. So, I offered to be a linesperson, it was much safer standing on the sidelines and I was included in the teas afterwards. A win-win situation!

My end of term report for once was quite favourable and at last my poor parents had a little hope for me. Wendy had joined the school the previous year and I frequently heard, "Why can't you be more like your sister?" from exasperated members of staff.

Conversely, Wendy was told thankfully and with great surprise, "You're nothing like your sister, thank goodness."

It didn't exactly make for sisterly relationships and to my shame, I ignored her for most of the time.

Chapter 18

Alas, the next term I reverted to type. We were joined by our pupils from junior school and the teasing and bullying restarted. Luckily my new friends, Pam, Cynthia, Jean, Meg and Davina were not part of the regime although, they stayed on the sidelines and didn't get involved at all. Julia wasted no time asserting her superiority over us all and as usual I was her whipping boy.

That year, we had 'domestic skills' on the syllabus. We were divided into three groups for needlework, cookery and art, one term at each. I started in the needlework group and the first session we were taught how to thread a Singer sewing machine. They were the old-fashioned models with a treadle. I managed to sew my finger into the machine when my foot slipped on the treadle and unfortunately, the blood seeped into the business area. It stopped working and I was dismissed from the lesson forthwith.

I was then sent to learn how to cook. I had missed the first session of theory and scone baking was on the agenda. Great! But I was unaware of the abbreviations in recipes and put two tablespoons of bicarb of soda instead of half a teaspoon into my scones. They rose like no others and I was complimented on their appearance. As the best scones were sent to the staffroom to be eaten, I felt cheated as the others were eating theirs there and then. The compliments soon turned to blame when numbers of staff had to hurriedly visit the toilets soon after they had tasted my lofty offerings. So, no more cookery that term.

The art class was the only option left. Again, I had missed the safety talk and arrived the day we started lino cutting. The inevitable happened, the knife slipped and there was blood over all the piece of lino. Matron was NOT pleased! In spite of such an unfortunate start, I stayed in the art class during that school year and as I really enjoyed the subject, it was a pleasure.

The next term Miss Arthur, the art mistress, suggested a mural painted along the whole of one art room wall. It was a magnificent project and we all set to with a will, painting a jungle scene and using our vivid imaginations. Come the last art lesson of term and it needed to be washed away. That entailed a lot of water splashing about and a murky grey wall appeared. I offered to stay behind and clean it, a relief from break time on my own and for the work I did, I was awarded the 'Musgrave prize for drawing' at the end of the year. We were expected to choose an erudite book on art but I asked for *Mrs Beeton's Cookery book*, which to my astonishment I received at the end of term assembly.

Chapter 19

"FIRE! FIRE!" came the shout. "Everyone to your stations." Excitement indeed. The summons came mid- morning in the middle of a very boring geography lesson – who wanted to learn the mountain ranges in the Urals by heart anyway? We duly filed out to the front lawn where we awaited the arrival of the local fire engine – and its complement of gorgeous young firemen!

This was the usual once a term fire practice to ensure the safety of the whole school. We had our own in-house fire service (wo)manned by upper school pupils who dashed about with hoses, hard hatted and sporting vivid yellow jackets. They were the heroines of the day and their goal was to arrive at the scene fully prepared to fight any fire before the brigade arrived. It looked wonderfully romantic and I determined to join the fire brigade at the first opportunity.

My chance came when I got into the lower 5th. At the end of the first gym lesson, Miss Peebles asked for volunteers to join the school fire brigade. This entailed one afternoon each week for training and it sounded fun. It was run by Miss Peebles and was taken very seriously.

The first afternoon, we learnt how to use the equipment. The head gardener was in-charge. Before he arrived in the fire shed, Miss Peebles gave us a timely warning. "Listen very carefully to Mr McGregor, it is very important," – pause to clear throat. "But if he says anything that you might find a little… er…embarrassing, please do not laugh."

We had no idea what she was talking about but couldn't wait for the instruction to begin.

After telling us what the various bits and pieces were for, Mr McGregor took two hoses, one in each hand and said gleefully, "You put the male into the female and you twist."

The last few words were drawn out and emphasised with attendant actions. We weren't sure what he meant but from the look on Miss Peeble's face we knew we weren't meant to snigger then! So of course, we did!

We became very proficient at getting the hoses out, connecting them to the main hydrant and aiming at an imaginary fire. Each term we timed ourselves against the local fire brigade, who rushed into the grounds with all sirens and lights at full strength, plus the gorgeous young firemen, of course.

Mr McGregor taught us the firemans' lift. He took great delight in picking each volunteer up, throwing us over his shoulder and holding onto the top of our legs very tightly whilst climbing the ladder. It did seem a little excessive to try it out on every girl but we were so innocent then... We had to practise carrying each other up and down ladders to the flat roof over the common room, not something that health and safety would endorse today.

A week after the official fire practice, the shout went up, "FIRE! FIRE!" The usual procedure was put into use. Fire monitors rang bells throughout the school and general exodus was put into action – practice made perfect!

Fire!

The brigade ran to the fire shed, donned hats and jackets and waited for Miss Peebles to tell us where the imaginary fire was. She did not appear. What should we do? The possibility of fighting a real fire had not come into the equation and we were at a loss.

Swift action was called for. Tessa, a 6th former and head of the fire brigade took charge. "We must find Miss Peebles," she said authoritatively. "She will know where the fire is."

We hauled all our gear to the front lawn where the whole school was assembled to see what was happening. Miss Sears took control of the collected throng.

"Who set off the fire alarm?" she asked, obviously thinking it was some sort of prank. I felt sure she looked at me but for once I was innocent.

A voice piped up from the back of the assembly. "I did, Miss Sears; I saw smoke and flames coming from the staff quarters so I thought I'd better ring the alarm."

Great! This was the real thing. We felt a frisson of excitement mixed with not a little fear that this might be a life or death situation, and ran with our equipment to the back door, the nearest access point to the source of the fire which was on the second floor which housed the staff quarters.

Fire in the staff quarters

We attached the hose to the hydrant in true professional manner and taking the other end, ran to the back staircase to get to the fire. We remembered to put the male into the female and twist, and swiftly ascended the spiral staircase to the second floor.

Unfortunately, the hose ran out just before the top step and there was no way we could reach the cause of the fire. This was just as well as it transpired that some clothes had fallen from a clothes horse onto an electric fire in one of the staff bedrooms and we would have done a great deal of mischief had we doused the element with gallons of water. In any case, the fire brigade had forestalled us and had already made the situation safe.

The fireman in charge looked at four sweaty, panting, yellow-coated, hard-hatted teenagers and smiled patiently.

"If you had brought the hose straight up the centre of the spiral staircase instead of up the steps with you, it would have reached the fire," he said kindly, adding, "perhaps next time you could use this." He pointed to a neatly coiled fire hose on the wall ready for action. We retreated hastily but were hailed as heroes by the school. We did not let on that we hadn't actually put the fire out ourselves and Miss Peebles said nothing to the contrary. In future sessions, we were shown how to attack fires from inside the school should the occasion ever arise. Talking about shutting the stable door.

Chapter 20

The bullying became insidious rather than physical. I was never picked for a side at netball practice and was totally ignored when it was my turn to pick a team. The one time I was given that honour, all my team played for the opponents' side. My games kit was either 'mislaid' or stuffed behind the lockers where I might have left it, but hadn't. Eventually this came to the notice of members of staff and they kept a wary eye on me but from a distance. Nothing was done to stop the teasing; it was deemed character building and I was left to cope on my own.

Pam was always sympathetic but as with many of the class was in awe of Julia and her cronies and couldn't or wouldn't stand up to them. She advised me to go along with what they wanted as it would make life a lot easier. It didn't!

Above our classroom was a balcony. It led to the staffroom and was definitely out of bounds. It held several interesting shaped boxes and I was dared to climb up the lockers, over the balustrade and report on my findings.

"Go on, Judy, you're good at climbing, you'll find out what's there," exhorted Julia. She and the gang were so enthusiastic about my gymnastic abilities and sense of adventure that I almost felt accepted as part of their coterie, so I reluctantly agreed, the locker unit was pushed under the balcony and up I went.

I scrambled up the lockers and over the balustrade amid cheers from below. This was music to my ears and I revelled in my new-found popularity. I whipped off the dustsheet covers expecting heaven knows what underneath.

"It's only blankets here," I called down in great disappointment.

"Look under them, there might be a body," came the cry from below. I did. Absolutely nothing there, not a severed arm, headless torso or any other gruesome object!

"I'm ready to come down now," I shouted, ready to descend. The minute I had my leg over the railing and was feeling for the locker top, the locker was wrenched away from the wall and I was left stranded.

At that moment, the lesson bell went, the class teacher came to register attendance and of course, I was absent. Nobody had seen me, no one knew where I was and there I stayed until break when Julia and the gang had gone, no doubt giggling at the thought of my discomfiture and possible later punishment. Pam was the only one who stayed behind and singlehandedly struggled to move the lockers and I was able to come down to earth. So much for trying to gain a little popularity.

Chapter 21

It was becoming obvious that life at school was not my forte and eventually the staff took action. The following term instead of sleeping in a dormitory with 19 others, I was placed in a room at 'Hightrees', a house opposite the main building which housed small numbers of pupils who would benefit from more individual attention. I would be in a room with just two other girls and it would be a little more like home.

What a change! Miss Coombes who ran it was a lovely motherly soul who I really took to, and both behaviour and work improved tremendously. On the quiet, she helped me tidy my drawers, make the bed with proper hospital corners and most importantly, gave me her time. She also said she loved Bruiny, which really endeared her to me. By the end of term, I actually got top marks for tidiness and won the house cup – much to the astonishment of everyone, not least Miss Barmite, who actually thought I had fiddled the marks.

House cup for tidiness

The following term, deemed to be 'cured' of my bad behaviour, I was returned to the main building, under the care of Miss Barmite. We had dormitory inspection every Monday morning, so Sunday evenings were a mad dash to clean and tidy our cubicles. I really tried my hardest to be tidy, my hospital corners were a wonder to behold, but no matter how hard I tried I never got more than 10 out of 20 each week. I felt it was most unfair so Cynthia, in the next bed, and I hatched out a plan to prove that I was being victimised. She didn't like Miss Barmite either, although she was obsessively tidy and always got full marks each week.

For the next month, she kept my cubicle clean and tidy and I looked after hers. And each week hers got 20 out of 20 and mine got a measly 10. After four weeks, we asked to see Miss Barmite. We presented her with a copy of the marks and demanded an explanation for her duplicity. NOT A GOOD IDEA! We were both accused of deceitfulness, cheek and disrespect towards a member of staff which we thought was most unfair. We actually took our complaint to Miss Sears, the Headmistress. Whilst privately sympathising with us, she pointed out that there was a right and a wrong way to complain and ours was definitely not a wise course of action. It might have unforeseen consequences. She was absolutely right; we were definitely in Miss Barmite's bad books from then on.

Chapter 22

Notice on school notice board.

'HAVE YOU GOT GREEN FINGERS?
DO YOU LIKE GARDENING?

There are some garden plots available near by the tennis courts for anyone who would like to take over one and make a beautiful show. An ideal hobby for the summer term. Plants available from Mr McGregor.

Prize for the best garden awarded at the end of term.

For details please contact the staffroom.'

Pam and I read the notice eagerly. We found we had similar interests and as both our parents were keen gardeners, we had learnt the basics and enjoyed it. There was also the inducement of a prize, actually it was the main inducement, so in due course we were the proud possessors of a square of weeds and nettles. Actually, we were the only ones who took up the offer, so naturally we won the prize at the end of the summer. Both lots of parents were delighted. At last, I was applying myself to something useful.

Proud possessor of a square of weeds

We talked a lot while we were digging out weeds and roots. Pam really wanted a penfriend and had put in a plea in the columns of all the magazines we avidly devoured each week. Nothing came of it and she became very upset at the thought that nobody wanted to get in touch. Cynthia and I got quite worried about her, she had stopped eating, withdrew into her shell and was most unlike herself.

We thought we had the perfect answer. We would reply to her plea and be the penfriend she wanted. All details were worked out. To make it even more interesting, the writer would be a boy which would give Pam great street cred.

We invented a short life history for him, which we would improvise on later as things progressed. His name was Martin Phillips and he was two years older than Pam, they had similar interests and it sounded perfect. Cynthia had an aunt who lived in Pinner and she was inveigled to accept any post to Martin and return it to Cynthia in a separate envelope. Pam and I always opened our letters together, so it was no good sending them to me.

She was delighted with the first letter that came. Her mood lightened and she showed the letter to all her friends with great enthusiasm. Cynthia and I had taken the precaution to keep this subterfuge from the rest of the class, we must have known deep down that it was a sneaky thing to do but we thought the end justified the means. We helped Pam pen a suitable reply and the correspondence continued regularly.

Naturally, the deceit had to come to light eventually and it was Julia once more who was in the forefront. Instead of getting rid of 'Martin's' letters, we had kept them so we could keep tabs on what he had written and wouldn't tie ourselves up in a lie – that's a laugh in itself, the whole thing was a lie from the start to finish but we thought we were so clever.

We weren't prepared for Julia to go turn out our lockers, where we kept all our private bits and pieces. None of the lockers had locks, we were taught the importance of trust and nothing ever went missing. But it wasn't unknown for them to be rifled through just for the fun of it and the few friends I had made were fair game for teasing along with me and routinely had desks and lockers messed up.

Julia found the incriminating letters and immediately cottoned on to us. The next break, she and her cronies collared us in the lavatory block, confronted us with the pile of letters and threatened us with exposure not only to Pam, to all members of staff and our parents, but also to the police for false impersonation. She also demanded all our spending money and sweets. She made a very effective blackmailer and we were terrified. She gave us 24 hours to come up with the sweets and money or all would be revealed. It was an Agatha Christie situation come to life and we were at a loss to know how to deal with it.

We begged, we pleaded, we sobbed and we cowered. They laughed in our faces and Julia repeated the demand menacingly. We begged even more, they sniggered at our humiliation and stalked off. How could we get out of this predicament?

We decided tearfully to come clean to Pam. It was not an easy decision and an even harder thing to confess. She took the news very badly, it was the deceit that upset her the most, the fact that we only did it to make her happy was entirely ignored and sadly it was the end of a lovely friendship – and a gardening partner. It was also thank goodness, the end of Julia's attempt at blackmail, but Cynthia and I learnt a salutary lesson and Martin Philips was no more.

Chapter 23

Cynthia and I had remained good friends after the letter debacle. We both came in for our share of teasing and bullying but it wasn't so bad when there were two of us.

She wanted to come and visit in the summer holidays. She had never been north of Birmingham, that I couldn't imagine, but 'The North' was a foreign country to most of the class.

My mother, always doing the right thing – wish I had learnt from her…wrote to Cynthia's parents inviting their daughter for a holiday with us. Imagine her chagrin on reading the reply.

'Dear Mrs Snelling,
Thank you for inviting Cynthia to stay with you during the summer holidays, but we wouldn't dream of letting her go so far north on her own.'
She added, *'After all we do have running water and proper toilets down here.'*

Mum was furious, Cynthia was mortified that her mother had said that and her parents were very cool towards me when we met at speech day later that term. I had so looked forward to showing my friend our beautiful county, the moors and dales, the desolate expanse of Spurn point by the mighty river Humber, but all our pleading fell on deaf ears and her parents were still convinced we lived like savages.

Chapter 24

May, morning assembly, great hall.

"This evening," started Miss Sears. "You will all be delighted to hear Mr Yale is coming to give us his yearly current affairs lecture."

We weren't.

He was an elderly, bald man with a go-to-sleep voice, which did not carry further than the first t w o rows. We were expected to listen carefully to all he droned on about.

We didn't.

We were expected to write an essay the next day on the interesting things he had spoken about.

We couldn't!

Summer term was the season for evening lectures. Some were boring (but not as boring as Mr Yale's). Some were interesting but very few were memorable.

One such was a man from the Foreign Office, an actual spy in the war and he was fascinating. He brought various artefacts with him which he passed around for us to examine. We couldn't find the secret message in the fountain pen or the code in his tiepin, and his wristwatch which was also a compass and Morse code transmitter was a complete mystery to us all.

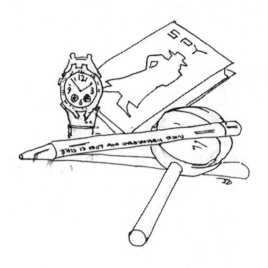

Secret message in a fountain pen

I was enthralled, and decided there and then that I would be a spy when I left school. It seemed such a brave and heroic calling and I wasn't even put off with his story about the spy who had his head shaved and tattooed with a complex chemical formula. He then had to wait till his hair grew before disappearing into enemy territory to find his opposite number and have his head shaved once more to extract the information from his scalp. What happened to him in later life if he went bald was not mentioned!

Not one to waste time, I wrote off to the Foreign office, addressed the letter and envelope to 'The Chief Spy, Whitehall, London', giving every scrap of information which I thought might get me a job. A m a z i n g l y , my application reached someone there and I had a very civilised letter back.

'Dear Judy,

Thank you for your application to work with us as an agent. We have your details on file. We are sure that your ability to finish the Telegraph crossword will stand you in good stead for a code-breaking career but feel that you will need a little more experience of life before we can offer you a future in the service. We advise you to finish your education and we will be happy to consider you in the future.

Yours sincerely.'

Naturally, I took that as a yes. My career plans solved, I stopped worrying about exams as nothing was mentioned about qualifications in their letter. I also stopped worrying about handing in homework on time... They just wanted me to finish my education and this I resolved to do at the earliest opportunity! My father had other ideas though and soon put paid to my Marta Hari dreams and brought me back down to earth with a stern lecture.

The school prefects were an unapproachable bunch. They patrolled the corridors at break, oversaw our table manners, and were generally aloof and officious to us minors. They complained that we had no manners and needed a good talking to. They got more than they bargained for. Miss Sears invited one of the ladies in waiting at court – not Julia's distant relation thank goodness – to come and give a lecture to the whole school on manners.

It was extremely illuminating... We learnt how to address an archbishop and members of the royal family. We were taught how to eat cream meringues with a cake fork whilst wearing white elbow length gloves at Buckingham Palace and how to fill in a dance card at a formal ball, plus many other niceties which I have long since forgotten. All completely useless to a lass from Yorkshire with no leaning to attend a palace garden party or play hostess to an archbishop.

Chapter 25

There was a special announcement at morning assembly at the start of the summer term by Miss Pearce, the music teacher.

"This year's Gilbert and Sullivan musical will be 'The Gondoliers'. It will be performed at Parents' Day at the end of term and there will be auditions for anyone interested in taking part after dinner this evening in the hall."

First of all, I wondered, who were Gilbert and Sullivan and what was the musical she had mentioned? This had escaped my prior education and I admitted my ignorance when we got back to the form room. Big mistake!

"You ignorant, stupid goat," said Julia. "Everybody knows who they are."

"Of course, you're from up north," chimed in Sarah. "It's no wonder, you've no culture at all up there."

"Stupid Poo," added Lisa.

"You really ought to audition," said Helen. "You're just the sort they need." At this, all four collapsed into fits of giggles, turned their backs on me as usual and ignored me for the rest of the evening. Luckily, Cynthia filled me in on G & S, as they were affectionately known, and I was a little wiser by bedtime.

As I couldn't sing a note in tune, there was no way I could audition for anything so stayed well away from the hall that evening. It transpired however that the producer was also looking for backstage personnel to make scenery, paint backcloths and be a general dogsbody and there were very few applicants for such a menial task.

I loved it! As far as I was concerned, the success of the whole production rested entirely on my shoulders. If the props were in the wrong place, if the lights failed at a crucial time and it was a total disaster, it would be my fault and nobody else's. To that end, I was super diligent, super-efficient and had a total disregard for any schoolwork I should have done.

In the event, it was a crowning success. The scenery didn't fall down, the homemade gondolier glided across the stage at strategic times with only a slight hiccup when it ran over an actor's foot and all the backstage staff were congratulated on their hard work.

That was it! I was destined to be on the stage – or behind it, I wasn't fussy either way, as long as I could be involved with the theatre. I took part in all future drama activities and actually had a speaking part in 'The Merchant of Venice'. That was very special as my parents came to that particular speech day and I could show them just what a budding thespian I was.

Over afternoon tea, I announced proudly that I knew what career I wanted and I was prepared to work really hard to achieve my ambition.

"What is it, darling?" asked Mum eagerly. My father looked a little dubious, perhaps he knew my propensity for work-shyness better than I did!

"I'm going to be an actress," I said confidently looking them both straight in the eye. You would have thought I had stated that I was destined for a life of crime with a murder or two thrown in for good measure. Father spluttered over his cup of lukewarm tea, almost choked, and was momentarily lost for words.

"You've gone and upset your father, dear," said Mum reproachfully whilst he got his breath back and launched into a fierce tirade on the vulgarity of 'those people' who were no better than they ought to be and what they get up to in those dreadful digs was anybody's guess. He ended by declaiming that no daughter of his was going to demean herself so far and I had better think again.

Wow! That took the wind out of my sails completely and for a moment, I was tempted to defy him and argue my case. But in the 1950s, it was just not done to defy parents and sulking was a much more insidious and effective action. They never came to see me in a play after that which was a great disappointment. Mind you, they were probably quite right, I wasn't much good although very eager and would have made a really good gofer, if nothing else!

Chapter 26

Leading on from my abortive drama aspirations, I grabbed any excuse to perform in whatever area was wanted. The following term the Music Cup competition took place between the schoolhouses.

Everyone was expected to take part, a song was chosen by Miss Pearce for each house and we were sent off to various rooms to rehearse under the watchful eye – and ear – of our housemistress. As Miss Barmite had no ear at all for music and wasn't interested in music per se, we were left to our own devices to arrange and perform the song in two parts.

Nelson must have been the most tuneless house for years and no one had much idea of part singing. Luckily, Pam learnt the piano and by dint of looking at the sheet music was able to fathom out some sort of harmony.

The song chosen could possibly not have been worse. All the other houses had a British folk song to learn. We were given 'The Teddy Bears' Picnic', no doubt thinking that it wouldn't matter if we ruined it for the audience.

Due to my enthusiasm for standing up and making a fool of myself in public, and also that I couldn't sing in tune, it was decided that I would be the conductor and general organiser. I knew we hadn't a chance of winning the cup, so Pam and I went out to be entertaining rather than musical. Pam was accompanying the choir on the piano.

The afternoon of the competition arrived. We were the last on and marvelled at the dulcet tones of 'Early one morning', 'Charlie is my darling' and 'Green grow the rushes O'. Where the 'Teddy bears' picnic' fitted in I shall never know but it was what was allocated and we must do our best.

I strode onto the stage and stood at the podium, baton in hand, and introduced proudly, "Nelson house choir will now present 'The teddy bears' picnic'." I ended this short speech with a flourish and Bruiny was produced from behind my back holding a miniature basket of food. Cheers and laughter from the floor!

The choir then entered, hands demurely behind their backs and smiling nervously at the audience. I turned to them and mouthed, "SMILE." They did! I held my baton up, ready for action and at a nod from me, the whole choir produced a teddy bear complete with picnic basket from behind their backs. More cheers from the floor.

Teddy bears' picnic

We will draw a veil over the actual singing performance, but the dancing bears were a hit. They twisted and twirled in unison, which is more than the song did, and the audience loved every moment. We got the loudest applause and the lowest marks, but the adjudicator said it was a performance she would never forget. That was good enough for us.

Chapter 27

"Your spots are revolting," sneered Julia, peering over my shoulder as I peered into the mirror in horror. Where did they suddenly appeared from? We had got to the age where Nivea cream was the panacea for all skin ailments and we blathered our faces with it night and morning.

Julia was right, they were disgusting. And they itched. "Bed bugs," intoned Julia. "For goodness sake, stay away from me." I was only too willing to!

Then she began to scratch too. "Bed bugs?" I asked innocently as she found a nasty spot on her cheek. She glared at me and I continued scratching my own itches. They got worse and I began to feel distinctly queasy.

It wasn't long before a great number of us came out with the same symptoms and chickenpox was diagnosed. The school came to a full stop and we all took to our beds.

Imagine over 100 girls sick and itching with high temperatures and occasionally vomiting in inappropriate places and it's no wonder matron felt like tearing her hair out. The school sanatorium had 23 beds, so only the more seriously affected were admitted, the rest were isolated into dormitories on the top floor in the vain hope that those unaffected would escape the illness. It was a forlorn hope however and the spots and itches spread rapidly.

It coincided with our preparation for confirmation. The school had its own chapel, services were held there each day and at the age of 13, we were all expected to retake our baptismal vows. It was quite a momentous occasion. Apart from the obvious religious significance, we all had a special white dress for the occasion and even better, we got presents. We were such a mercenary lot!

My timing as always was atrocious. My spots arrived two days before the confirmation service. My parents were coming to school for the occasion, one of their few visits and there was no way I was going to miss that. I refused to take to my bed and valiantly soldiered on.

Not for long though, I managed to faint at the last rehearsal with a very high temperature and was rushed off to the san where they found me a spare bed on my own in a disused linen room. Whether my reputation had gone before me, I will never know but I felt so ill I didn't care. Let the service go ahead, I was far too busy scratching all over to relieve the itching and crying because I thought my parents weren't coming.

The following day, Miss Sears came to visit. What had I done wrong now? She only saw me when I was in trouble.

"Don't sit up," she said kindly, as she sat on the side of the bed.

I couldn't anyway, she was sitting on my foot.

"We have organised things for you tomorrow."

I had no idea what she was talking about and must have looked dumb. She continued. "The bishop is willing to come and confirm you here. There is another girl who is being confirmed and he will do you both together. And yes, your parents are still coming and you won't miss out on the celebration dinner afterwards."

Dinner be blowed, I couldn't imagine ever eating again but cheered up at the thought of seeing Mum and Dad. They duly arrived, with my beautiful white dress wrapped in tissue paper and Mum helped me dress for the occasion.

It seemed as though a miracle had happened. The nursing staff had transformed the largest ward in the san into a chapel. They had wheeled all the beds in with all the other spottees, everything was white and there was even an altar at the end of the ward. I was wheeled into the ward in a chair and waited for the other girl to arrive and the service to start.

To my horror, it was Julia who was wheeled in and placed beside me. She looked even worse than I did and the expression on her face made her look even more horrific. It had been stressed at confirmation class that our partner at the service would be our great friend for life. Not a chance there.

The bishop of St Albans was an elderly, lovely man but he suffered very badly with the shakes and he pressed very hard on every single spot on my head when he blessed me. It was agony and I'm afraid that the true significance of the service passed me by. I wasn't even well enough to enjoy the feast that was laid on afterwards. I desperately wanted to go home with my parents but was deemed too ill to travel. That was probably a wise decision but they had to come back and take me home 10 days later and I was sick in the car all the way up the A1. My father was not pleased, dry sick is not the easiest stuff to wipe off car upholstery after a six-hour journey.

Chapter 28

I recovered quickly at home. Christmas came and I was given a speedometer for my bike as a present. Naturally, I had to try it out. It didn't work until the bike got up to a speed of 15mph, a fact that my father was unaware or he wouldn't have bought it. Luckily, the roads were empty when I fell off onto my wrist and ended up in hospital for a minor operation.

Returning to school with suitcase, shoulder bag and Bruiny was a struggle. I had my arm in a garish silk sling provided by my mother. Bruiny travelled in the sling, only falling out twice and I had help from our escorting mistress. As it was my right hand in the sling my written work for that term was in left hand shorthand – which meant that I couldn't decipher much of the term's work, a spider could have written more clearly.

"Judy, your turn for mug duty," called the class monitor disregarding my one-armed status.

During winter terms, we were given a mug of cocoa and a sticky bun at morning break. I really enjoyed being on duty, dishing out the drinks and buns. There were inevitably some left and we looked on them as a rightful bonus.

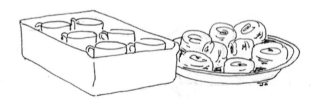

Cocoa and sticky buns

I didn't want to relinquish my duty – and the sticky buns – so went to collect the box of mugs from the kitchen. Not an easy task singlehanded and as I took them off the table, the box fell from my grasp and landed, the right way up, on the tone floor. Satisfied that nothing had broken I left them and went for the bun tray.

Lunchtime came. We filed into the dining room and took our places. Shock horror! That box of mugs stood in the middle of the serving table for all to see. What on earth had gone wrong? I was soon to find out.

Miss Sears said grace and we sat. She stood, looking sternly around. "We have a serious situation here," she began. "Someone has been throwing mugs around and hiding the broken ones under the others. This is a deceitful action as well as vandalism. Will the culprit please own up at once?"

My face felt scarlet with shame. My hand shot up. I was sitting to one side of Miss Sears and she did not see me. She demanded again. "Will the girl who did this please own up? Otherwise, the whole school will be punished." I waved frantically, she still missed me. The school didn't.

"It's Judy Snelling," several of them chorused gleefully. Miss Sears noticed me, made me stand up in front of the whole school and demanded a full explanation.

"It was an accident," I said. "I was on mug duty and they slipped from my hand. I didn't realise any had broken or I would have told someone." (A little white lie never goes amiss.)

She looked at my sling, admonished the monitor for letting me carry them, then to my astonishment I was held up as a shining example of honesty and complimented on my bravery for owning up. WOW!

I didn't get the same accolade from Matron who berated me for possibly harming my hand, or from Miss Barmite who just thought I was an idiot for carrying them in the first place. She would as usual, inform my parents of my stupid action.

"Not before I do," I muttered under my breath and immediately wrote a heartfelt letter home to explain everything. It must have worked! I received a letter the next week with a pound note enclosed to offer to pay for the damage. I felt that honesty only went so far, nobody asked for any payment and I was certainly not going to offer any.

Chapter 29

"It's your turn Judy, Miss Sears will see you now." Not in trouble this time but a talk about our future after O' Levels the next term.

I had no idea what my future might be, I had enough trouble coping with the present to worry about so I went with an open mind and expected her to tell me what to do with my life. A career as a spy was not an option and as for going on the stage, the less said about that the better.

I got a salutary shock. Miss Sears handed me a sheet of paper and told me to read the contents. She had asked for comments from other staff members and the results made illuminating reading – if you liked horror stories…

"If Judy put as much effort into her schoolwork as she does in disrupting the class, she would do much better." Geography.

"Judy has great ability but has no idea how to harness it." History.

"Judy is a poor influence on her fellow pupils and must curb her rebellious spirit." English.

"Judy is untidy and unhelpful and her attitude leaves a lot to be desired." Miss Barmite, naturally!

At last a positive report. "Judy is an asset to the team and is a natural leader. We are pleased to have her in the fire brigade." Miss Peebles.

There were others all of the same unflattering bent. They were much the same as I had on my reports every term, so I was not unduly surprised.

"You are such a disappointment, Judy," said Miss Sears. "We expected much better from you."

I mumbled, "Sorry, Miss Sears," not quite sure I meant it but felt I had to say something.

"If you are really sorry, you'll do something about it," she replied. "Doing a bit of work and passing an exam or two would be a start." She sighed heavily and continued. "I really don't think we can do much for you here. You can stay until after your exams but we don't want you back after that."

"Do you really mean that?" I asked breathlessly.

"Yes, of course, I always mean what I say. I must add that you are the very first girl I have had to expel in all my years of teaching, but there is no way we can allow you to continue here."

I grabbed her hand in gratitude, "Thank you so much, Miss Sears, I really appreciate that." She was startled to say the least. I think it was the first time anybody had been pleased to be expelled. She hastily terminated the interview and called in the next pupil.

My parents were remarkably sanguine about my unexpected (?) early departure. Or maybe they had seen the writing on the wall. In any event, they put on a brave face at all the money and time I had wasted over the past s e v e n years and we had an earnest discussion on what career I might be suited for.

Mum suggested I might like a nursing career. I had been given a first aid kit for my seventh birthday and was a dab hand at bandaging dolls and teddies. It was only one step further to patching up people in her eyes. I neglected to mention that I couldn't stand the sight of blood and it was decided that I would apply to the local children's hospital for training.

Amazingly, I was accepted and returned to school with a completely different mindset. I was leaving – Hurrah! I had a job with training to go to – even better! And I would leave Julia and her crowd behind as a bad memory. Best of all…

I thought I had better do some work for a change. I would have to buckle down in my chosen profession – or rather, Mum's chosen choice of career for me, so I ought to get used to studying.

I applied myself with a will. We were not allowed books in the dormitories, (can't think why not) and staff were on the lookout for anyone who tried to smuggle books upstairs hidden under jumpers. I found it much easier to carry a pile of books in full view and was never questioned where I was taking them. Perhaps the staff were so amazed I was actually studying that they left me alone.

Exams came and went in the usual fashion. Rows of desks were laid out in the main hall, large SILENCE AT ALL TIMES notices were prominently displayed. We crammed in frantic last-m i n u t e revision 10 minutes before we filed into the hall, various acronyms hidden on our wrists to remind us of facts we might need.

THEN – the very last day of term arrived, my very last term with my very last end of term report to come. Other girls who were leaving and not going into the 6th form were upset and crying at the thought of not seeing all their friends again. I thought I ought to cry with them but couldn't bring myself to be hypocritical. I couldn't wait to leave.

Chapter 30

Celebration! My very last day, last breakfast, last train to Euston and on to home. As usual, Bruiny was with me. No amount of teasing would persuade me not to have him travelling in my arm.

Although we had officially left school when we went through the gates, we still had to wear full school uniform all the way home. This included the dreaded berets with their ridiculous tassels. Mine was once again stitched in place after yet another try from Julia to hurl the beret as far as it would go.

Waiting at the platform at Watford station, I was aware of Julia close behind my shoulder. The train was due in two minutes. She had put down her case and was closing in on me ready to snatch my tassel and no doubt throw it as far as possible.

I side stepped her. She saw the feint and moved likewise. We dodged around each other like a couple of boxers. I ducked left, she twisted right and tripped over her case. It fell. Not only did it fall, it tumbled onto the track, the lid burst open and the contents were strewn over the electric lines and sleepers.

All was chaos. Whistles blew, guards appeared from out of the woodwork and one quick thinking official tried to extricate her belongings from the track with a sweeping brush. Julia stood horrified as her lacy bra was stuck on the bristles and waved around for all the world to see.

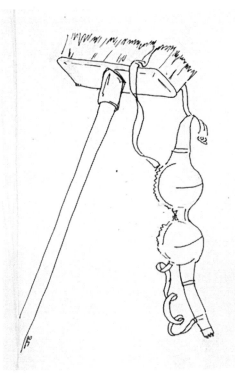

Lacy bra on bristles

"Whose belongings are these?" asked an irate station master arriving on the scene. We all scattered to the ladies' room. Julia was left to face the music. In the nick of time, the lines were cleared, the train arrived and the rest of us hurriedly boarded the 3rd class carriage.

Julia was escorted away held by two burly railway policemen. We never saw her again; she missed her train and possibly lost her belongings. There is justice in this world after all.

Julia was led away

Epilogue

The year is 2019.

I am 79 and 3/4 years old.

What did I bring away from my seven years away at boarding school? The following memories come to mind. They are as clear as daylight even after all these years.

A complete inability to decide when to go to bed. Until the age of 16, I had never stayed up later than 9:30 p.m. and only went to bed when told. It seems unbelievable now but I took it as the norm then.

A bolshie attitude to unnecessary rules. They are meant to be broken!

Unfortunately, for many years, a dislike of walks. They were meted out as punishment and it wasn't until I was much older that I appreciated walking the northern hills with family and dogs.

An obstinacy which stood me in good stead when I was teased. I didn't let the b...rs get me down!

An inability to feel at ease with boys! That didn't last all that long but I had to kiss a lot of frogs before I met my prince. After 59 years of marriage, he is still my prince – together with four children, assorted dogs, rabbits, guinea pigs, gerbils, mice, frogs, stick insects, crickets (to feed the lizards), Archibald, the drake with no feet and his harem, and two pet turkeys. And people think we are unconventional, can't think why!

AND – I passed all my O' Levels exams!!! Much to everyone's astonishment. I went back to my old day school to take A' Levels, and ended up working for the probation service, trying to help other social misfits – I felt great empathy with them…

P.S. Bruiny is still with me, sleeping peacefully on our bed each day. After all he is a VERY old bear!